DIET
JOURNAL
FOR
WOMEN
100 DAYS

....

....

ISBN-13: 978-1542461771
ISBN-10: 1542461774

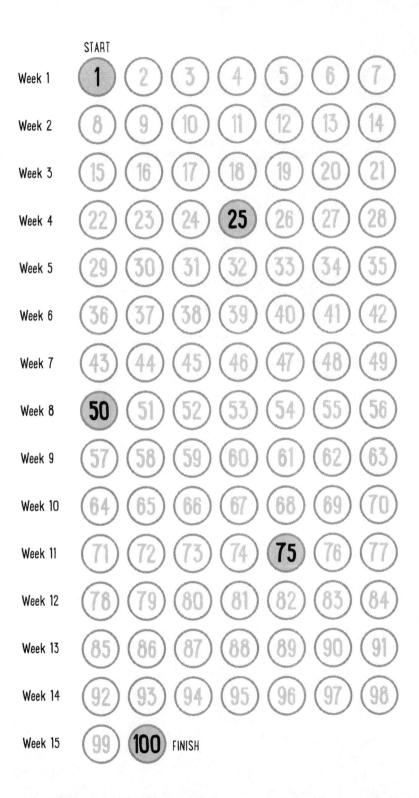

Day

My Measurements

.... Arm

.... Chest

.... Waist

.... Belly

.... Butt

.... Thigh

.... Calf

Weight

My Goals

Day (1)

Mo Tu We Th Fr Sa Su

Date ....

Emotional State

○   ○   ○   ○

Breakfast	Lunch	Dinner
....	....	....
....	....	....
....	....	....
....	....	....
....	....	....
....	....	....
‾‾‾‾‾‾‾‾‾‾ ‾‾‾‾	....	....
Snacks	....	....
....	....	....
....	....	....
....	....	....
....	....	....
....	....	....
‾‾‾‾‾‾‾‾‾‾‾‾ ‾‾‾‾	‾‾‾‾‾‾‾‾‾‾‾‾ ‾‾‾‾	‾‾‾‾‾‾‾‾‾‾‾‾ ‾‾‾‾

Total Calories

‾‾‾‾‾‾‾‾‾‾‾‾‾‾‾‾‾‾‾‾

Weight

Sleep   #Times Awake   Water   Protein

Exercise/Activity   Set / Reps   Time

....
....
....
....
....
....

Emotional State

Mo Tu We Th Fr Sa Su

Date ....

Day (2)

Breakfast
....
....
....
....
....
....
_____ _____

Snacks
....
....
....
....
....
_____ _____

Lunch
....
....
....
....
....
....
....
....
....
....
....
....
....
_____ _____

Dinner
....
....
....
....
....
....
....
....
....
....
....
....
_____ _____

Total Calories
_____

Weight

Sleep #Times Awake Water Protein

Exercise/Activity	Set / Reps	Time
....	....	....
....	....	....
....	....	....
....	....	....
....	....	....
....	....	....

Day ③

Mo Tu We Th Fr Sa Su

Date ....

Emotional State

○   ○   ○   ○

Breakfast	Lunch	Dinner
....	....	....
....	....	....
....	....	....
....	....	....
....	....	....
....	....	....
_____ ____	....	....
Snacks	....	....
....	....	....
....	....	....
....	....	....
....	....	....
....	....	....
_____ ____	_____ ____	_____ ____

Total Calories

_____

Weight ....

Sleep ....

#Times Awake ....

Water ....

Protein ....

♡ Exercise/Activity

	Set / Reps	Time
....	....	....
....	....	....
....	....	....
....	....	....
....	....	....
....	....	....

Emotional State

Mo Tu We Th Fr Sa Su

Date ....

Day ④

Breakfast
....
....
....
....
....
....

Snacks
....
....
....
....
....

Lunch
....
....
....
....
....
....
....
....
....
....
....
....
....

Dinner
....
....
....
....
....
....
....
....
....
....
....

Total Calories
_____

Weight

Sleep	#Times Awake	Water	Protein

❤ Exercise/Activity	Set / Reps	Time
....	....	....
....	....	....
....	....	....
....	....	....
....	....	....
....	....	....

Day (5)

Mo Tu We Th Fr Sa Su

Date ....

Emotional State

Breakfast	Lunch	Dinner
....	....	....
....	....	....
....	....	....
....	....	....
....	....	....
....	....	....
_____ _____	....	....
Snacks	....	....
....	....	....
....	....	....
....	....	....
....	....	....
....	....	....
_____ _____	_____ _____	_____ _____

Total Calories
_____

Weight

Sleep   #Times Awake   Water   Protein

....

❤ **Exercise/Activity**   Set / Reps   Time

.... | .... | ....
.... | .... | ....
.... | .... | ....
.... | .... | ....
.... | .... | ....

Emotional State

Mo Tu We Th Fr Sa Su

Date ....

Day

Breakfast

....
....
....
....
....
....

Snacks

....
....
....
....
....

Lunch

....
....
....
....
....
....
....
....
....
....
....
....
....
....
....

Dinner

....
....
....
....
....
....
....
....
....
....
....

Total Calories
_____

Weight

Sleep	#Times Awake	Water	Protein
....	....	....	....

Exercise/Activity

	Set / Reps	Time
....	....	....
....	....	....
....	....	....
....	....	....
....	....	....
....	....	....

Day (7)

Mo Tu We Th Fr Sa Su

Date ....

Emotional State

Breakfast	Lunch	Dinner
....	....	....
....	....	....
....	....	....
....	....	....
....	....	....
....	....	....

Snacks

....
....
....
....
....

Total Calories

_____

Weight

Sleep   **#Times Awake**   **Water**   **Protein**

Exercise/Activity   **Set / Reps**   **Time**

....
....
....
....
....
....

Emotional State

Mo Tu We Th Fr Sa Su

Date ....

Breakfast	Lunch	Dinner
....	....	....
....	....	....
....	....	....
....	....	....
....	....	....
....	....	....
	....	....

Snacks

....	....	....
....	....	....
....	....	....
....	....	....
....	....	....

Total Calories
_____

Weight

Sleep   #Times Awake   Water   Protein

Exercise/Activity   Set / Reps   Time

....	....	....
....	....	....
....	....	....
....	....	....
....	....	....
....	....	....

Day ⑨

Mo Tu We Th Fr Sa Su

Date ....

Emotional State

Breakfast	Lunch	Dinner
....	....	....
....	....	....
....	....	....
....	....	....
....	....	....
....	....	....
_____ _____	....	....
Snacks	....	....
....	....	....
....	....	....
....	....	....
....	....	....
....	....	....
_____ _____	_____ _____	_____ _____

Total Calories

_____

Weight

Sleep   #Times Awake   Water   Protein

Exercise/Activity

	Set / Reps	Time
....	....	....
....	....	....
....	....	....
....	....	....
....	....	....
....	....	....

Emotional State

Mo Tu We Th Fr Sa Su

Date ....

Day (10)

Breakfast

....
....
....
....
....
....
_____

Snacks

....
....
....
....
....
_____

Lunch

....
....
....
....
....
....
....
....
....
....
....
....
_____

Dinner

....
....
....
....
....
....
....
....
....
....
....
_____

Total Calories

_____

Weight

Sleep   #Times   Water   Protein
             Awake

....

Exercise/Activity   Set / Reps   Time

....
....
....
....
....
....

Day (11)

Mo Tu We Th Fr Sa Su

Date ....

Emotional State

😀 ○ 🙂 ○ 😐 ○ ☹ ○

Breakfast	Lunch	Dinner
....	....	....
....	....	....
....	....	....
....	....	....
....	....	....
....	....	....
_____ ___	....	....
Snacks	....	....
....	....	....
....	....	....
....	....	....
....	....	....
....	....	....
_____ ___	_____ ___	_____ ___

Total Calories

_____

Weight

Sleep   #Times
             Awake

Water   Protein

⏰ .... 🌙 ....   🥛 ....   🧴 ....

❤️‍🩹 Exercise/Activity   Set / Reps   Time

	Set / Reps	Time
....	....	....
....	....	....
....	....	....
....	....	....
....	....	....
....	....	....

Emotional State

Mo Tu We Th Fr Sa Su

Date ....

Day (12)

Breakfast	Lunch	Dinner
....	....	....
....	....	....
....	....	....
....	....	....
....	....	....
....	....	....
	....	....
Snacks	....	....
....	....	....
....	....	....
....	....	....
....	....	....
....	....	....

Total Calories
_____

Weight

Sleep   #Times Awake   Water   Protein

Exercise/Activity

	Set / Reps	Time
....	....	....
....	....	....
....	....	....
....	....	....
....	....	....
....	....	....

Day (13)

Mo Tu We Th Fr Sa Su

Date ....

Emotional State

Breakfast

....
....
....
....
....
....

Snacks

....
....
....
....
....

Lunch

....
....
....
....
....
....
....
....
....
....
....
....
....
....
....
....

Dinner

....
....
....
....
....
....
....
....
....
....
....
....
....
....
....

Total Calories

_____

Weight

Sleep   #Times
             Awake

Water   Protein

Exercise/Activity   Set / Reps   Time

....
....
....
....
....
....

Emotional State

Mo Tu We Th Fr Sa Su

Date ....

Day (14)

Breakfast
....
....
....
....
....
....

Snacks
....
....
....
....
....

Lunch
....
....
....
....
....
....
....
....
....
....
....
....
....
....
....

Dinner
....
....
....
....
....
....
....
....
....
....
....
....
....
....

Total Calories
_____

Weight

Sleep ....

#Times Awake ....

Water

Protein ....

Exercise/Activity   Set / Reps   Time
.... | .... | ....
.... | .... | ....
.... | .... | ....
.... | .... | ....
.... | .... | ....
.... | .... | ....

Day (15)

Mo Tu We Th Fr Sa Su

Date ....

Emotional State

Breakfast	Lunch	Dinner
....	....	....
....	....	....
....	....	....
....	....	....
....	....	....
....	....	....

Snacks

....	....	....
....	....	....
....	....	....
....	....	....
....	....	....

Total Calories
_____

Weight

Sleep #Times Awake Water Protein

Exercise/Activity

Set / Reps   Time

....
....
....
....
....

Emotional State

Mo Tu We Th Fr Sa Su

Date ....

Day (16)

Breakfast	Lunch	Dinner
....	....	....
....	....	....
....	....	....
....	....	....
....	....	....
....	....	....

Snacks

....
....
....
....
....

Total Calories
_____

Weight

Sleep   #Times Awake   Water   Protein

Exercise/Activity   Set / Reps   Time

.... | .... | ....
.... | .... | ....
.... | .... | ....
.... | .... | ....
.... | .... | ....
.... | .... | ....

Day (17)

Date ....

Mo Tu We Th Fr Sa Su

Emotional State

Breakfast
....
....
....
....
....
....
_____ _____

Snacks
....
....
....
....
....
_____ _____

Lunch
....
....
....
....
....
....
....
....
....
....
....
....
....
....
....
....
_____ _____

Dinner
....
....
....
....
....
....
....
....
....
....
....
....
....
....
....
....
....
_____ _____

Total Calories
_____

Weight

Sleep .... #Times Awake .... Water .... Protein ....

Exercise/Activity   Set / Reps   Time

.... | .... | ....
.... | .... | ....
.... | .... | ....
.... | .... | ....
.... | .... | ....
.... | .... | ....

Emotional State

Mo Tu We Th Fr Sa Su

Date ....

Day (18)

Breakfast	Lunch	Dinner
....	....	....
....	....	....
....	....	....
....	....	....
....	....	....
....	....	....

Snacks

....
....
....
....
....

Total Calories

_____

Weight

Sleep   #Times Awake   Water   Protein

Exercise/Activity   Set / Reps   Time

....
....
....
....
....
....

Day (19)

Mo Tu We Th Fr Sa Su

Date ....

Emotional State

Breakfast

....
....
....
....
....
....

Snacks

....
....
....
....
....

Total Calories

Lunch

....
....
....
....
....
....
....
....
....
....
....
....
....

Dinner

....
....
....
....
....
....
....
....
....
....
....
....
....

Weight

Sleep ....

#Times Awake ....

Water

Protein ....

Exercise/Activity

Exercise/Activity	Set / Reps	Time
....	....	....
....	....	....
....	....	....
....	....	....
....	....	....
....	....	....

Emotional State

Mo Tu We Th Fr Sa Su

Date ....

Day

Breakfast

....
....
....
....
....
....

Snacks

....
....
....
....
....

Lunch

....
....
....
....
....
....
....
....
....
....
....
....
....

Dinner

....
....
....
....
....
....
....
....
....
....
....
....

Total Calories

_____

Weight

Sleep   #Times
             Awake

Water   Protein

Exercise/Activity   Set / Reps   Time

....
....
....
....
....
....

Day (21)

Mo Tu We Th Fr Sa Su

Date ....

Emotional State

Breakfast	Lunch	Dinner
....	....	....
....	....	....
....	....	....
....	....	....
....	....	....
....	....	....

Snacks

.... | ....

.... | ....

.... | ....

.... | ....

.... | ....

Total Calories

_____

Weight

Sleep   #Times Awake   Water   Protein

Exercise/Activity

	Set / Reps	Time
....	....	....
....	....	....
....	....	....
....	....	....
....	....	....

Emotional State

Mo Tu We Th Fr Sa Su

Date ....

Day (22)

Breakfast

....
....
....
....
....
....

Snacks

....
....
....
....
....

Lunch

....
....
....
....
....
....
....
....
....
....
....
....
....

Dinner

....
....
....
....
....
....
....
....
....
....
....
....
....

Total Calories

_____

Weight

Sleep .... #Times Awake .... Water .... Protein ....

Exercise/Activity | Set / Reps | Time

Exercise/Activity	Set / Reps	Time
....	....	....
....	....	....
....	....	....
....	....	....
....	....	....
....	....	....

Day (23)

Mo Tu We Th Fr Sa Su

Date ....

○ ○ ○ ○

Breakfast

....
....
....
....
....
....

_____ _____

Snacks

....
....
....
....
....

_____ _____

Lunch

....
....
....
....
....
....
....
....
....
....
....
....

Dinner

....
....
....
....
....
....
....
....
....
....
....

_____ _____

Total Calories

_____

Weight

Sleep

#Times Awake

Water

Protein

Exercise/Activity

Set / Reps   Time

.... | .... | ....
.... | .... | ....
.... | .... | ....
.... | .... | ....
.... | .... | ....
.... | .... | ....

Emotional State

Mo Tu We Th Fr Sa Su

Date ....

Day (24)

Breakfast	Lunch	Dinner
....	....	....
....	....	....
....	....	....
....	....	....
....	....	....
....	....	....

Snacks

....	....	....
....	....	....
....	....	....
....	....	....
....	....	....

Total Calories

_____

Weight

Sleep   **#Times Awake**   **Water**   **Protein**

Exercise/Activity   **Set / Reps**   **Time**

Exercise/Activity	Set / Reps	Time
....	....	....
....	....	....
....	....	....
....	....	....
....	....	....
....	....	....

Day (25)

Mo Tu We Th Fr Sa Su

Date ....

Emotional State

Breakfast

....
....
....
....
....
....
_____ _____

Snacks

....
....
....
....
....
_____ _____

Lunch

....
....
....
....
....
....
....
....
....
....
....
_____ _____

Dinner

....
....
....
....
....
....
....
....
....
....
....
_____ _____

Total Calories
_____

Weight

Sleep

#Times Awake

Water

Protein

Exercise/Activity

	Set / Reps	Time
....	....	....
....	....	....
....	....	....
....	....	....
....	....	....

My Measurements

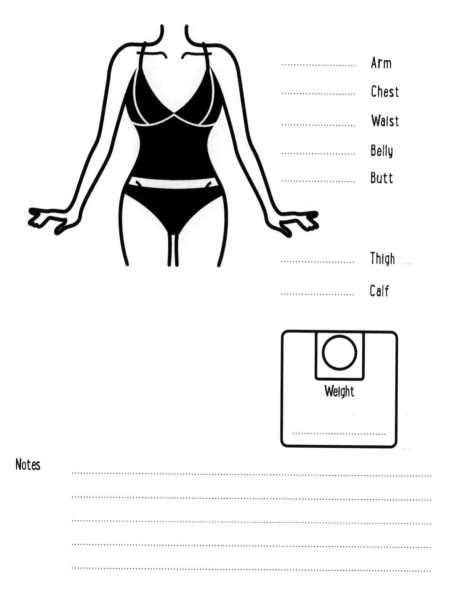

.... Arm

.... Chest

.... Waist

.... Belly

.... Butt

.... Thigh

.... Calf

Weight

....

Notes ....

....

....

....

....

Day (26)

Mo Tu We Th Fr Sa Su

Date ....

Emotional State

Breakfast

....
....
....
....
....
....
_____

Snacks

....
....
....
....
....
_____

Total Calories

_____

Weight

Sleep   #Times Awake   Water   Protein

Lunch

....
....
....
....
....
....
....
....
....
....
....
....
....
....

Dinner

....
....
....
....
....
....
....
....
....
....
....
....
....
....

Exercise/Activity   Set / Reps   Time

....
....
....
....
....
....

Emotional State

Mo Tu We Th Fr Sa Su

Date ....

Day (27)

Breakfast

....
....
....
....
....
....

Snacks

....
....
....
....
....

Lunch

....
....
....
....
....
....
....
....
....
....
....
....
....
....
....

Dinner

....
....
....
....
....
....
....
....
....
....
....
....
....

Total Calories

_____

Weight

Sleep	#Times Awake	Water	Protein

Exercise/Activity   Set / Reps   Time

....
....
....
....
....
....

Day (28)

Mo Tu We Th Fr Sa Su

Date ....

Emotional State

Breakfast

....
....
....
....
....
....

Snacks

....
....
....
....
....

Lunch

....
....
....
....
....
....
....
....
....
....
....
....
....

Dinner

....
....
....
....
....
....
....
....
....
....
....
....
....

Total Calories

_____

Weight

Sleep   #Times
             Awake

Water   Protein

Exercise/Activity   Set / Reps   Time

....
....
....
....
....

Emotional State

Mo Tu We Th Fr Sa Su

Date ....

Day (29)

Breakfast	Lunch	Dinner
....	....	....
....	....	....
....	....	....
....	....	....
....	....	....
....	....	....

Snacks

....

....

....

....

....

Total Calories
_____

Weight

Sleep   #Times Awake   Water   Protein

♡ Exercise/Activity   Set / Reps   Time

.... | .... | ....
.... | .... | ....
.... | .... | ....
.... | .... | ....
.... | .... | ....
.... | .... | ....

Day **30**

Date ....

Mo Tu We Th Fr Sa Su

Emotional State

Breakfast

....
....
....
....
....
....
_____ _____

Snacks

....
....
....
....
....
_____ _____

Lunch

....
....
....
....
....
....
....
....
....
....
....
....
....
_____ _____

Dinner

....
....
....
....
....
....
....
....
....
....
....
....
....
_____ _____

Total Calories

_____

Weight

Sleep #Times Awake Water Protein

Exercise/Activity

Set / Reps Time

Emotional State

Mo Tu We Th Fr Sa Su

Date ....

Day (31)

Breakfast	Lunch	Dinner
....	....	....
....	....	....
....	....	....
....	....	....
....	....	....
....	....	....

Snacks

....

....

....

....

....

Total Calories

_____

Weight

Sleep   #Times Awake   Water   Protein

Exercise/Activity   Set / Reps   Time

....

....

....

....

....

....

Day (32)

Mo Tu We Th Fr Sa Su

Date ....

Emotional State

Breakfast

....
....
....
....
....
....

Snacks

....
....
....
....
....

Total Calories

Weight

Lunch

....
....
....
....
....
....
....
....
....
....
....
....
....

Dinner

....
....
....
....
....
....
....
....
....
....
....
....
....

Sleep   #Times Awake   Water   Protein

Exercise/Activity   Set / Reps   Time

....
....
....
....
....
....

Emotional State

Mo Tu We Th Fr Sa Su

Date ....

Day (33)

Breakfast	Lunch	Dinner
....	....	....
....	....	....
....	....	....
....	....	....
....	....	....
....	....	....

Snacks

....
....
....
....
....

Total Calories

_____

Weight

Sleep   #Times Awake   Water   Protein

Exercise/Activity   Set / Reps   Time

.... | .... | ....
.... | .... | ....
.... | .... | ....
.... | .... | ....
.... | .... | ....
.... | .... | ....

Day (34)

Mo Tu We Th Fr Sa Su

Date ....

Emotional State

Breakfast

....
....
....
....
....
....

_____ _____

Snacks

....
....
....
....
....

_____ _____

Lunch

....
....
....
....
....
....
....
....
....
....
....
....

_____ _____

Dinner

....
....
....
....
....
....
....
....
....
....
....

_____ _____

Total Calories

_____

Weight

| Sleep | #Times Awake | Water | Protein |

Exercise/Activity

Set / Reps	Time
....	....
....	....
....	....
....	....
....	....

Emotional State

Mo Tu We Th Fr Sa Su

Date ....

Day (35)

Breakfast	Lunch	Dinner
....	....	....
....	....	....
....	....	....
....	....	....
....	....	....
....	....	....

Snacks

....
....
....
....
....

Total Calories
_____

Weight

Sleep #Times Awake Water Protein

Exercise/Activity   Set / Reps   Time

....
....
....
....
....
....

Day 36

Mo Tu We Th Fr Sa Su

Date ....

Emotional State

Breakfast

....
....
....
....
....
....
_____ _____

Snacks

....
....
....
....
....
_____ _____

Lunch

....
....
....
....
....
....
....
....
....
....
....
....
....
....
_____ _____

Dinner

....
....
....
....
....
....
....
....
....
....
....
....
....
....
_____ _____

Total Calories

_____

Weight

Sleep | #Times Awake | Water | Protein

Exercise/Activity | Set / Reps | Time

.... | .... | ....
.... | .... | ....
.... | .... | ....
.... | .... | ....
.... | .... | ....
.... | .... | ....

Emotional State

Mo Tu We Th Fr Sa Su

Date ....

Day (37)

Breakfast

....
....
....
....
....
....

Snacks

....
....
....
....
....

Total Calories
_____

Lunch

....
....
....
....
....
....
....
....
....
....
....
....
....

Dinner

....
....
....
....
....
....
....
....
....
....
....
....
....

Weight

Sleep   #Times Awake   Water   Protein

Exercise/Activity   Set / Reps   Time

....
....
....
....
....
....

Day (38)

Mo Tu We Th Fr Sa Su

Date ....

Emotional State

Breakfast	Lunch	Dinner
....	....	....
....	....	....
....	....	....
....	....	....
....	....	....
....	....	....
_____ ___	....	....
Snacks	....	....
....	....	....
....	....	....
....	....	....
....	....	....
....	....	....

Total Calories
_____

Weight

Sleep   #Times Awake   Water   Protein

Exercise/Activity   Set / Reps   Time

.... | .... | ....
.... | .... | ....
.... | .... | ....
.... | .... | ....
.... | .... | ....
.... | .... | ....

Emotional State

Mo Tu We Th Fr Sa Su

Date ....

Day **39**

Breakfast
....
....
....
....
....
....

Snacks
....
....
....
....
....

Lunch
....
....
....
....
....
....
....
....
....
....
....
....
....
....

Dinner
....
....
....
....
....
....
....
....
....
....
....
....
....
....

Total Calories

Weight

Sleep   #Times Awake   Water   Protein

Exercise/Activity	Set / Reps	Time
....	....	....
....	....	....
....	....	....
....	....	....
....	....	....
....	....	....

Day (40)

Mo Tu We Th Fr Sa Su

Date ....

Emotional State

Breakfast	Lunch	Dinner
....	....	....
....	....	....
....	....	....
....	....	....
....	....	....
....	....	....

Snacks

....
....
....
....
....

Total Calories
_____

Weight

Sleep

#Times Awake

Water

Protein

❤ Exercise/Activity   Set / Reps   Time

.... | .... | ....
.... | .... | ....
.... | .... | ....
.... | .... | ....
.... | .... | ....

Emotional State

Mo Tu We Th Fr Sa Su

Date ....

Day (41)

Breakfast

....
....
....
....
....
....

Snacks

....
....
....
....
....

Total Calories

_____

Weight

Lunch

....
....
....
....
....
....
....
....
....
....
....
....
....

Dinner

....
....
....
....
....
....
....
....
....
....
....
....
....

Sleep	#Times Awake	Water	Protein
....	....	....	....

Exercise/Activity Set / Reps Time

Exercise/Activity	Set / Reps	Time
....	....	....
....	....	....
....	....	....
....	....	....
....	....	....
....	....	....

Day (42)

Mo Tu We Th Fr Sa Su

Date ....

Emotional State

Breakfast

....
....
....
....
....
....
_____ _____

Snacks

....
....
....
....
....
_____ _____

Lunch

....
....
....
....
....
....
....
....
....
....
....
....
....
_____ _____

Dinner

....
....
....
....
....
....
....
....
....
....
....
....
....
_____ _____

Total Calories

_____

Weight

Sleep   #Times
             Awake

Water   Protein

Exercise/Activity   Set / Reps   Time

....
....
....
....
....
....

Emotional State

Mo Tu We Th Fr Sa Su

Date ....

Day (43)

Breakfast	Lunch	Dinner
....	....	....
....	....	....
....	....	....
....	....	....
....	....	....
....	....	....

Snacks

....	....	....
....	....	....
....	....	....
....	....	....
....	....	....

Total Calories

_____

Weight

Sleep #Times Awake Water Protein

Exercise/Activity   Set / Reps   Time

....	....	....
....	....	....
....	....	....
....	....	....
....	....	....
....	....	....

Day (44)

Mo Tu We Th Fr Sa Su

Date ....

Emotional State

○ ○ ○ ○

Breakfast	Lunch	Dinner
....	....	....
....	....	....
....	....	....
....	....	....
....	....	....
....	....	....
_____ ___	....	....

Snacks

....	....	....
....	....	....
....	....	....
....	....	....
....	....	....
_____ ___	_____ ___	_____ ___

Total Calories
_____

Weight

Sleep   #Times Awake   Water   Protein

....

Exercise/Activity

Exercise/Activity	Set / Reps	Time
....	....	....
....	....	....
....	....	....
....	....	....
....	....	....
....	....	....

Emotional State

Mo Tu We Th Fr Sa Su

Date ....

Day (45)

Breakfast

....
....
....
....
....
....

Snacks

....
....
....
....
....

Lunch

....
....
....
....
....
....
....
....
....
....
....
....

Dinner

....
....
....
....
....
....
....
....
....

Total Calories

Weight ....

Sleep ....

#Times Awake ....

Water ....

Protein ....

Exercise/Activity   Set / Reps   Time

....
....
....
....
....
....

Day (46)

Mo Tu We Th Fr Sa Su

Date ....

Emotional State

Breakfast

....
....
....
....
....
....

_____ _____

Snacks

....
....
....
....
....

_____ _____

Total Calories

_____

Lunch

....
....
....
....
....
....
....
....
....
....
....
....
....

_____ _____

Dinner

....
....
....
....
....
....
....
....
....
....
....
....
....

_____ _____

Weight

Sleep ....

#Times Awake ....

Water

Protein ....

♥ Exercise/Activity

	Set / Reps	Time
....	....	....
....	....	....
....	....	....
....	....	....
....	....	....
....		

Emotional State

Mo Tu We Th Fr Sa Su

Date ....

Day 47

Breakfast	Lunch	Dinner
....	....	....
....	....	....
....	....	....
....	....	....
....	....	....
....	....	....

Snacks

.... | .... | ....
.... | .... | ....
.... | .... | ....
.... | .... | ....
.... | .... | ....

Total Calories

_____

Weight

Sleep · #Times Awake · Water · Protein

Exercise/Activity	Set / Reps	Time
....	....	....
....	....	....
....	....	....
....	....	....
....	....	....
....	....	....

Day (48)

Mo Tu We Th Fr Sa Su

Date ....

Emotional State

○ ○ ○ ○

Breakfast

....
....
....
....
....
....

_____ _____

Snacks

....
....
....
....
....

_____ _____

Total Calories

_____

Lunch

....
....
....
....
....
....
....
....
....
....
....
....
....

_____ _____

Dinner

....
....
....
....
....
....
....
....
....
....
....
....
....

_____ _____

Weight

Sleep .... #Times Awake .... Water .... Protein ....

Exercise/Activity   Set / Reps   Time

....
....
....
....
....
....

Emotional State

Mo Tu We Th Fr Sa Su

Date ....

Day (49)

Breakfast

....
....
....
....
....
....

Snacks

....
....
....
....
....

Lunch

....
....
....
....
....
....
....
....
....
....
....
....
....
....

Dinner

....
....
....
....
....
....
....
....
....
....
....
....
....
....

Total Calories

_____

Weight

Sleep   #Times
            Awake

Water   Protein

Exercise/Activity   Set / Reps   Time

....
....
....
....
....
....

Day (50)

Mo Tu We Th Fr Sa Su

Date ....

Emotional State

Breakfast

....
....
....
....
....
....

Snacks

....
....
....
....
....

Total Calories

Lunch

....
....
....
....
....
....
....
....
....
....
....
....
....
....
....
....

Dinner

....
....
....
....
....
....
....
....
....
....
....
....
....
....

Weight

Sleep   #Times
           Awake

Water   Protein

Exercise/Activity   Set / Reps   Time

....
....
....
....
....
....

Day 50

My Measurements

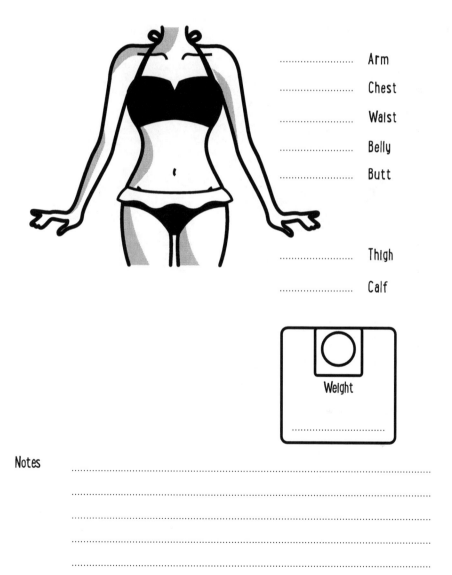

.... Arm

.... Chest

.... Waist

.... Belly

.... Butt

.... Thigh

.... Calf

Weight

....

Notes

Day (51)

Mo Tu We Th Fr Sa Su

Date ....

Emotional State

Breakfast
....
....
....
....
....
....
_____ _____

Snacks
....
....
....
....
....
_____ _____

Lunch
....
....
....
....
....
....
....
....
....
....
....
....
....
....
....
_____ _____

Dinner
....
....
....
....
....
....
....
....
....
....
....
....
....
....
_____ _____

Total Calories
_____

Weight

Sleep   #Times Awake   Water   Protein

Exercise/Activity   Set / Reps   Time
.... | .... | ....
.... | .... | ....
.... | .... | ....
.... | .... | ....
.... | .... | ....

Emotional State

Mo Tu We Th Fr Sa Su

Date ....

Day (52)

Breakfast
....
....
....
....
....
....
_____ _____

Snacks
....
....
....
....
....
_____ _____

Lunch
....
....
....
....
....
....
....
....
....
....
....
....
....
....
_____ _____

Dinner
....
....
....
....
....
....
....
....
....
....
....
....
....
....
_____ _____

Total Calories
_____

Weight

Sleep   #Times
            Awake

Water   Protein

Exercise/Activity   Set / Reps   Time
.... | .... | ....
.... | .... | ....
.... | .... | ....
.... | .... | ....
.... | .... | ....
.... | .... | ....

Day (53)

Date ....

Mo Tu We Th Fr Sa Su

○   ○   ○   ○

Breakfast

....
....
....
....
....
....

Snacks

....
....
....
....
....

Lunch

....
....
....
....
....
....
....
....
....
....
....
....
....
....

Dinner

....
....
....
....
....
....
....
....
....
....
....
....
....
....

Total Calories

_____

Weight

Sleep   #Times Awake   Water   Protein

🕐 ....   🌙 ....   🥛 ....   🧴 ....

♥ Exercise/Activity   Set / Reps   Time

.... | .... | ....
.... | .... | ....
.... | .... | ....
.... | .... | ....
.... | .... | ....
.... | .... | ....

Emotional State

Mo Tu We Th Fr Sa Su

Date ....

Day (54)

Breakfast	Lunch	Dinner
....	....	....
....	....	....
....	....	....
....	....	....
....	....	....
....	....	....

Snacks

Total Calories
_____

Weight

Sleep   #Times Awake   Water   Protein

Exercise/Activity   Set / Reps   Time

Day (55)

Mo Tu We Th Fr Sa Su

Date ....

Emotional State

○   ○   ○   ○

Breakfast	Lunch	Dinner
....	....	....
....	....	....
....	....	....
....	....	....
....	....	....
....	....	....
_____ __	....	....

Snacks

....	....	....
....	....	....
....	....	....
....	....	....
....	....	....

Total Calories

_____

Weight

Sleep   #Times Awake   Water   Protein

Exercise/Activity   Set / Reps   Time

	Set / Reps	Time
....	....	....
....	....	....
....	....	....
....	....	....
....	....	....

Emotional State

☺ ○ ☺ ○ 😐 ○ ☹ ○

Mo Tu We Th Fr Sa Su

Date ....

Day (56)

Breakfast	Lunch	Dinner
....	....	....
....	....	....
....	....	....
....	....	....
....	....	....
....	....	....
——————— ————	....	....

Snacks

....

....

....

....

....

——————— ————

Total Calories
————————————————

Weight

Sleep #Times Awake Water Protein

⏰ .... 🌙 .... 🥤 .... 🧴 ....

♥ Exercise/Activity   Set / Reps   Time

.... | .... | ....
.... | .... | ....
.... | .... | ....
.... | .... | ....
.... | .... | ....
.... | .... | ....

Day (57)

Mo Tu We Th Fr Sa Su

Date ....

Emotional State

○   ○   ○   ○

Breakfast	Lunch	Dinner
....	....	....
....	....	....
....	....	....
....	....	....
....	....	....
....	....	....

_____ ____

Snacks

....
....
....
....
....

_____ ____

_____ ____

Total Calories

_____

Weight

Sleep   #Times
Awake

Water   Protein

🕐 ....   🌙 ....

💓 Exercise/Activity

	Set / Reps	Time
....	....	....
....	....	....
....	....	....
....	....	....
....	....	....
....	....	....

Emotional State

Mo Tu We Th Fr Sa Su

Date ....

Day (58)

Breakfast

....
....
....
....
....
....
_____ _____

Snacks

....
....
....
....
....
_____ _____

Lunch

....
....
....
....
....
....
....
....
....
....
....
....
....
....
....
_____ _____

Dinner

....
....
....
....
....
....
....
....
....
....
....
....
....
....
....
_____ _____

Total Calories
_____

Weight

Sleep   #Times Awake   Water   Protein

♥ Exercise/Activity   Set / Reps   Time

.... | .... | ....
.... | .... | ....
.... | .... | ....
.... | .... | ....
.... | .... | ....
.... | .... | ....

Day (59)

Mo Tu We Th Fr Sa Su

Date ....

Emotional State

Breakfast	Lunch	Dinner
....	....	....
....	....	....
....	....	....
....	....	....
....	....	....
....	....	....
_____ _____	....	....
Snacks	....	....
....	....	....
....	....	....
....	....	....
....	....	....
....	....	....
_____ _____	_____ _____	_____ _____

Total Calories

_____

Weight

Sleep   #Times Awake   Water   Protein

❤ **Exercise/Activity**   Set / Reps   Time

	Set / Reps	Time
....	....	....
....	....	....
....	....	....
....	....	....
....	....	....
....	....	....

Emotional State

Mo Tu We Th Fr Sa Su

Date ....

Day (60)

Breakfast

....
....
....
....
....
....

—————————— ————

Snacks

....
....
....
....
....

—————————— ————

Lunch

....
....
....
....
....
....
....
....
....
....
....
....
....
....
....

—————————— ————

Dinner

....
....
....
....
....
....
....
....
....
....
....
....

—————————— ————

Total Calories

——————————————

Weight

Sleep ....

#Times Awake ....

Water ....

Protein ....

Exercise/Activity | Set / Reps | Time

.... | .... | ....
.... | .... | ....
.... | .... | ....
.... | .... | ....
.... | .... | ....
.... | .... | ....

Day (61)

Mo Tu We Th Fr Sa Su

Date ....

Emotional State

Breakfast	Lunch	Dinner
....	....	....
....	....	....
....	....	....
....	....	....
....	....	....
....	....	....

Snacks

....
....
....
....
....

Total Calories

_____

Weight

Sleep   #Times Awake   Water   Protein

Exercise/Activity   Set / Reps   Time

....
....
....
....
....

Emotional State

Mo Tu We Th Fr Sa Su

Date ....

Day (62)

Breakfast

....
....
....
....
....
....
_____ _____

Snacks

....
....
....
....
....
_____ _____

Lunch

....
....
....
....
....
....
....
....
....
....
....
....
....
_____ _____

Dinner

....
....
....
....
....
....
....
....
....
....
....
....
....
_____ _____

Total Calories
_____

Weight

Sleep .... #Times Awake .... Water .... Protein ....

Exercise/Activity   Set / Reps   Time

....
....
....
....
....
....

Day (63)

Mo Tu We Th Fr Sa Su

Date ....

Emotional State

○ ○ ○ ○

Breakfast	Lunch	Dinner
....	....	....
....	....	....
....	....	....
....	....	....
....	....	....
....	....	....
_____ ____	....	....
Snacks	....	....
....	....	....
....	....	....
....	....	....
....	....	....
_____ ____	....	_____ ____

Total Calories
_____

Weight ....

Sleep ....

#Times Awake ....

Water ....

Protein ....

Exercise/Activity

	Set / Reps	Time
....	....	....
....	....	....
....	....	....
....	....	....
....	....	....
....	....	....

Emotional State

Mo Tu We Th Fr Sa Su

Date ....

Day (64)

Breakfast

....
....
....
....
....
....
_____ _____

Snacks

....
....
....
....
....
_____ _____

Lunch

....
....
....
....
....
....
....
....
....
....
....
....
....
_____ _____

Dinner

....
....
....
....
....
....
....
....
....
_____ _____

Total Calories
_____

Weight
....

Sleep ....

#Times Awake ....

Water ....

Protein ....

Exercise/Activity   Set / Reps   Time

.... | .... | ....
.... | .... | ....
.... | .... | ....
.... | .... | ....
.... | .... | ....
.... | .... | ....

Day (65)

Mo Tu We Th Fr Sa Su

Date ....

Breakfast

....
....
....
....
....
....
_____   _____

Snacks

....
....
....
....
....
_____   _____

Lunch

....
....
....
....
....
....
....
....
....
....
....
....
....
....
....
_____   _____

Dinner

....
....
....
....
....
....
....
....
....
....
....
....
_____   _____

Total Calories
_____

Weight	Sleep	#Times Awake	Water	Protein
	....	....	....	....

♥ Exercise/Activity

	Set / Reps	Time
....	....	....
....	....	....
....	....	....
....	....	....
....	....	....
....	....	....

Emotional State

Mo Tu We Th Fr Sa Su

Date ....

Day (66)

Breakfast	Lunch	Dinner
....	....	....
....	....	....
....	....	....
....	....	....
....	....	....
....	....	....
_____ ____	....	....

Snacks

Total Calories
_____

Weight

Sleep

#Times Awake

Water

Protein

Exercise/Activity

Set / Reps

Time

Day (67)

Mo Tu We Th Fr Sa Su

Date ....

Emotional State

◯ ◯ ◯ ◯

Breakfast
....
....
....
....
....
....

_____ _____

Snacks
....
....
....
....
....

_____ _____

Lunch
....
....
....
....
....
....
....
....
....
....
....
....
....

_____ _____

Dinner
....
....
....
....
....
....
....
....
....
....
....
....

_____ _____

Total Calories
_____

Weight

Sleep   #Times Awake   Water   Protein

♥ Exercise/Activity

	Set / Reps	Time
....	....	....
....	....	....
....	....	....
....	....	....
....	....	....
....	....	....

Emotional State

Mo Tu We Th Fr Sa Su

Date ....

Day (68)

Breakfast	Lunch	Dinner
....	....	....
....	....	....
....	....	....
....	....	....
....	....	....
....	....	....
_____ _____	....	....
Snacks	....	....
....	....	....
....	....	....
....	....	....
....	....	....
....	....	....
_____ _____	_____ _____	_____ _____

Total Calories

_____

Weight

Sleep   #Times Awake   Water   Protein

Exercise/Activity   Set / Reps   Time

Day (69)

Mo Tu We Th Fr Sa Su

Date ....

Breakfast

....
....
....
....
....
....

_____ _____

Snacks

....
....
....
....
....

_____ _____

Lunch

....
....
....
....
....
....
....
....
....
....
....
....
....

_____ _____

Dinner

....
....
....
....
....
....
....
....
....
....
....

_____ _____

Total Calories

_____

Weight

Sleep   **#Times Awake**   **Water**   **Protein**

....

♥ Exercise/Activity

	Set / Reps	Time
....	....	....
....	....	....
....	....	....
....	....	....
....	....	....
....	....	....

Emotional State

Mo Tu We Th Fr Sa Su

Date ....

Day **70**

Breakfast

....
....
....
....
....
....
_____ _____

Snacks

....
....
....
....
....
_____ _____

Lunch

....
....
....
....
....
....
....
....
....
....
....
....
....
....
....
....
_____ _____

Dinner

....
....
....
....
....
....
....
....
....
_____ _____

Total Calories
_____

Weight

Sleep   #Times Awake   Water   Protein

....

♡ Exercise/Activity

	Set / Reps	Time
....	....	....
....	....	....
....	....	....
....	....	....
....	....	....
....	....	....

Day (71)

Mo Tu We Th Fr Sa Su

Date ....

Emotional State

○   ○   ○   ○

Breakfast	Lunch	Dinner
....	....	....
....	....	....
....	....	....
....	....	....
....	....	....
....	....	....
_____ ____	....	....
Snacks	....	....
....	....	....
....	....	....
....	....	....
....	....	....
....	....	....
_____ ____	_____ ____	_____ ____

Total Calories
_____

Weight

Sleep   #Times Awake   Water   Protein

Exercise/Activity   Set / Reps   Time

....	....	....
....	....	....
....	....	....
....	....	....
....	....	....
....	....	....

Emotional State

Mo Tu We Th Fr Sa Su

Date ....

Day (72)

Breakfast	Lunch	Dinner
....	....	....
....	....	....
....	....	....
....	....	....
....	....	....
....	....	....
_____ ___	....	....
Snacks	....	....
....	....	....
....	....	....
....	....	....
....	....	....
....	....	....
_____ ___	_____ ___	_____ ___

Total Calories

_____

Weight ....

Sleep ....

#Times Awake ....

Water ....

Protein ....

Exercise/Activity

	Set / Reps	Time
....	....	....
....	....	....
....	....	....
....	....	....
....	....	....
....	....	....

Day (73)

Mo Tu We Th Fr Sa Su

Date ....

Emotional State

Breakfast	Lunch	Dinner
....	....	....
....	....	....
....	....	....
....	....	....
....	....	....
....	....	....
_____ ____	....	....

Snacks

....

....

....

....

....

_____ ____   _____ ____   _____ ____

Total Calories

_____

Weight

Sleep   #Times Awake   Water   Protein

Exercise/Activity   Set / Reps   Time

....	....	....
....	....	....
....	....	....
....	....	....
....	....	....
....	....	....

Emotional State

Mo Tu We Th Fr Sa Su

Date ....

Day (74)

Breakfast	Lunch	Dinner
....	....	....
....	....	....
....	....	....
....	....	....
....	....	....
....	....	....
_____ _____	....	....

Snacks

....

....

....

....

....

_____ _____

Total Calories

_____

 Weight ....

Sleep	#Times Awake	Water	Protein
....	....	....	....

 Exercise/Activity | Set / Reps | Time

	Set / Reps	Time
....	....	....
....	....	....
....	....	....
....	....	....
....	....	....
....	....	....

Day (75)

Date ....

Mo Tu We Th Fr Sa Su

Emotional State

○   ○   ○   ○

Breakfast	Lunch	Dinner
....	....	....
....	....	....
....	....	....
....	....	....
....	....	....
....	....	....
———————— ———	....	....
Snacks	....	....
....	....	....
....	....	....
....	....	....
....	....	....
....	....	....
———————— ———	———————— ———	———————— ———

Total Calories

————————————————

Weight

Sleep #Times Awake Water Protein

Exercise/Activity   Set / Reps   Time

....	....	....
....	....	....
....	....	....
....	....	....
....	....	....
....	....	....

My Measurements

.... Arm

.... Chest

.... Waist

.... Belly

.... Butt

.... Thigh

.... Calf

Weight

....

Notes

....

....

....

....

....

Day (76)

Mo Tu We Th Fr Sa Su

Date ....

Emotional State

○   ○   ○   ○

Breakfast

....
....
....
....
....
....

Snacks

....
....
....
....

Total Calories

Lunch

....
....
....
....
....
....
....
....
....
....
....
....

Dinner

....
....
....
....
....
....
....
....
....

Weight

Sleep   #Times Awake   Water   Protein

....

Exercise/Activity   Set / Reps   Time

....
....
....
....
....
....

Emotional State

Mo Tu We Th Fr Sa Su

Date ....

Day (77)

Breakfast	Lunch	Dinner
....	....	....
....	....	....
....	....	....
....	....	....
....	....	....
....	....	....

Snacks

....	....	....
....	....	....
....	....	....
....	....	....
....	....	....

Total Calories

Weight

Sleep #Times Awake Water Protein

Exercise/Activity	Set / Reps	Time
....	....	....
....	....	....
....	....	....
....	....	....
....	....	....
....	....	....

Day (78)

Mo Tu We Th Fr Sa Su

Date ....

Emotional State

○   ○   ○   ○

Breakfast

....
....
....
....
....
....
_____ _____

Snacks

....
....
....
....
....
_____ _____

Lunch

....
....
....
....
....
....
....
....
....
....
....
....
....
_____ _____

Dinner

....
....
....
....
....
....
....
....
....
....
....
....
....
_____ _____

Total Calories

_____

Weight

Sleep	#Times Awake	Water	Protein
....	....	....	....

♡ **Exercise/Activity**   Set / Reps   Time

.... | .... | ....
.... | .... | ....
.... | .... | ....
.... | .... | ....
.... | .... | ....
.... | .... | ....

Emotional State

😀 ⃝ 🙂 ⃝ 😐 ⃝ 🙁 ⃝

Mo Tu We Th Fr Sa Su

Date ....

Day (79)

Breakfast	Lunch	Dinner
....	....	....
....	....	....
....	....	....
....	....	....
....	....	....
....	....	....
_____ ____	....	....
Snacks	....	....
....	....	....
....	....	....
....	....	....
....	....	....
....	....	....
_____ ____	_____ _____	_____ ____

Total Calories
_____

Weight

Sleep ⏰ ....

#Times Awake 🌙 ....

Water ....

Protein ....

♥ Exercise/Activity

	Set / Reps	Time
....	....	....
....	....	....
....	....	....
....	....	....
....	....	....
....	....	....

Day (80)

Mo Tu We Th Fr Sa Su

Date ....

Emotional State

○   ○   ○   ○

Breakfast	Lunch	Dinner
....	....	....
....	....	....
....	....	....
....	....	....
....	....	....
....	....	....
_____ ____	....	....
Snacks	....	....
....	....	....
....	....	....
....	....	....
....	....	....
....	....	....
_____ ____	_____ ____	_____ ____

Total Calories

_____

Weight

Sleep   #Times Awake   Water   Protein

....

Exercise/Activity

	Set / Reps	Time
....	....	....
....	....	....
....	....	....
....	....	....
....	....	....
....	....	....

Emotional State

😃 ○ 😊 ○ 😐 ○ 🙁 ○

Mo Tu We Th Fr Sa Su

Date ....

Day **81**

Breakfast

....
....
....
....
....
....

_____ _____

Snacks

....
....
....
....
....

_____ _____

Lunch

....
....
....
....
....
....
....
....
....
....
....
....
....
....

_____ _____

Dinner

....
....
....
....
....
....
....
....
....
....
....
....
....
....

_____ _____

Total Calories

_____

Weight ....

Sleep	#Times Awake	Water	Protein
....	....	....	....

♥ Exercise/Activity   Set / Reps   Time

	Set / Reps	Time
....	....	....
....	....	....
....	....	....
....	....	....
....	....	....
....	....	....

Day (82)

Mo Tu We Th Fr Sa Su

Date ....

Emotional State

Breakfast	Lunch	Dinner
....	....	....
....	....	....
....	....	....
....	....	....
....	....	....
....	....	....
_____ __	....	....
Snacks	....	....
....	....	....
....	....	....
....	....	....
....	....	....
....	....	....

Total Calories
_____

Weight

Sleep   #Times Awake   Water   Protein

Exercise/Activity   Set / Reps   Time

....
....
....
....
....
....

Emotional State

Mo Tu We Th Fr Sa Su

Date ....

Day **83**

Breakfast

....
....
....
....
....
....
_____ _____

Snacks

....
....
....
....
....
_____ _____

Total Calories
_____

Lunch

....
....
....
....
....
....
....
....
....
....
....
....
....
....
....
_____ _____

Dinner

....
....
....
....
....
....
....
....
....
....
....
....
....
....
_____ _____

Weight

Sleep   #Times Awake   Water   Protein

Exercise/Activity	Set / Reps	Time
....	....	....
....	....	....
....	....	....
....	....	....
....	....	....
....	....	....

Day (84)

Mo Tu We Th Fr Sa Su

Date ....

Emotional State

Breakfast	Lunch	Dinner
....	....	....
....	....	....
....	....	....
....	....	....
....	....	....
....	....	....
_____ _____	....	....
Snacks	....	....
....	....	....
....	....	....
....	....	....
....	....	....
....	....	....
_____ _____	_____ _____	_____ _____

Total Calories
_____

Weight

Sleep   #Times Awake   Water   Protein

Exercise/Activity   Set / Reps   Time

....
....
....
....
....
....

Emotional State

:D :) :| :(

Mo Tu We Th Fr Sa Su

Date ....

Day (85)

Breakfast

....
....
....
....
....
....

_____ ___

Snacks

....
....
....
....
....

_____ ___

Lunch

....
....
....
....
....
....
....
....
....
....
....
....
....

_____ ___

Dinner

....
....
....
....
....
....
....
....
....
....
....

_____ ___

Total Calories

_____

Weight ....

	Sleep	#Times Awake	Water	Protein

Exercise/Activity | Set / Reps | Time

.... | .... | ....
.... | .... | ....
.... | .... | ....
.... | .... | ....
.... | .... | ....
.... | .... | ....

Day (86)

Mo Tu We Th Fr Sa Su

Date ....

Emotional State

Breakfast	Lunch	Dinner
....	....	....
....	....	....
....	....	....
....	....	....
....	....	....
....	....	....

Snacks

....	....	....
....	....	....
....	....	....
....	....	....
....	....	....

Total Calories
_____

Weight

Sleep   #Times Awake   Water   Protein

Exercise/Activity   Set / Reps   Time

	Set / Reps	Time
....	....	....
....	....	....
....	....	....
....	....	....
....	....	....
....	....	....

Emotional State

Mo Tu We Th Fr Sa Su

Date ....

Day (87)

Breakfast

....
....
....
....
....
....
_____ _____

Snacks

....
....
....
....
....
_____ _____

Lunch

....
....
....
....
....
....
....
....
....
....
....
....
....
....
....
_____ _____

Dinner

....
....
....
....
....
....
....
....
....
....
....
....
....
....
....
_____ _____

Total Calories

_____

Weight

Sleep   #Times Awake   Water   Protein

Exercise/Activity

	Set / Reps	Time
....	....	....
....	....	....
....	....	....
....	....	....
....	....	....
....	....	....

Day (88)

Mo Tu We Th Fr Sa Su

Date ....

Emotional State

O   O   O   O

Breakfast

....
....
....
....
....
....
_____ _____

Snacks

....
....
....
....
....
_____ _____

Lunch

....
....
....
....
....
....
....
....
....
....
....
....
....
_____ _____

Dinner

....
....
....
....
....
....
....
....
....
....
....
....
....
_____ _____

Total Calories

_____

Weight

Sleep #Times Awake Water Protein

Exercise/Activity   Set / Reps   Time

....
....
....
....
....
....

Emotional State

Mo Tu We Th Fr Sa Su

Date ....

Day **89**

Breakfast

....
....
....
....
....
....

_____ _____

Snacks

....
....
....
....
....

_____ _____

Lunch

....
....
....
....
....
....
....
....
....
....
....
....
....

_____ _____

Dinner

....
....
....
....
....
....
....

_____ _____

Total Calories

_____

Weight

Sleep	#Times Awake	Water	Protein
....	....	....	....

Exercise/Activity

	Set / Reps	Time
....	....	....
....	....	....
....	....	....
....	....	....
....	....	....
....	....	....

Day (90)

Mo Tu We Th Fr Sa Su

Date ....

Emotional State

Breakfast	Lunch	Dinner
....	....	....
....	....	....
....	....	....
....	....	....
....	....	....
....	....	....
_____ ____	....	....
Snacks	....	....
....	....	....
....	....	....
....	....	....
....	....	....
....	....	....
_____ ____	_____ ____	_____ ____

Total Calories

_____

Weight

Sleep   #Times Awake   Water   Protein

Exercise/Activity   Set / Reps   Time

....

....

....

....

....

....

Emotional State

Mo Tu We Th Fr Sa Su

Date ....

Day (91)

Breakfast	Lunch	Dinner
....	....	....
....	....	....
....	....	....
....	....	....
....	....	....
....	....	....
_____ ____	....	....
Snacks	....	....
....	....	....
....	....	....
....	....	....
....	....	....
....	....	....
_____ ____	_____ ____	_____ ____

Total Calories
_____

Weight

Sleep   #Times Awake   Water   Protein

....

Exercise/Activity   Set / Reps   Time

....	....	....
....	....	....
....	....	....
....	....	....
....	....	....
....		

Day (92)

Mo Tu We Th Fr Sa Su

Date ....

Emotional State

Breakfast	Lunch	Dinner
....	....	....
....	....	....
....	....	....
....	....	....
....	....	....
....	....	....
	....	....
Snacks	....	....
....	....	....
....	....	....
....	....	....
....	....	....
....	....	....

Total Calories
_____

Weight

Sleep   #Times
               Awake

Water   Protein

....

Exercise/Activity   Set / Reps   Time

....

....

....

....

....

....

Emotional State

Mo Tu We Th Fr Sa Su

Date ....

Day (93)

Breakfast	Lunch	Dinner
....	....	....
....	....	....
....	....	....
....	....	....
....	....	....
....	....	....

Snacks

....

....

....

....

....

Total Calories
_____

Weight

Sleep   #Times Awake   Water   Protein

Exercise/Activity

Exercise/Activity	Set / Reps	Time
....	....	....
....	....	....
....	....	....
....	....	....
....	....	....
....	....	....

Day (94)

Mo Tu We Th Fr Sa Su

Date ....

Emotional State

Breakfast	Lunch	Dinner
....	....	....
....	....	....
....	....	....
....	....	....
....	....	....
_____ _____	....	....
Snacks	....	....
....	....	....
....	....	....
....	....	....
....	....	....
....	....	....
_____ _____	_____ _____	_____ _____

Total Calories

_____

Weight

....

	Sleep	#Times Awake	Water	Protein

....

❤ Exercise/Activity

	Set / Reps	Time
....	....	....
....	....	....
....	....	....
....	....	....
....	....	....
....	....	....

Emotional State

Mo Tu We Th Fr Sa Su

Date ....

Day (95)

Breakfast	Lunch	Dinner
....	....	....
....	....	....
....	....	....
....	....	....
....	....	....
....	....	....
_____ _____	....	....

Snacks

....	....	....
....	....	....
....	....	....
....	....	....
....	....	....
_____ _____	_____ _____	_____ _____

Total Calories

_____

Weight

Sleep   #Times Awake   Water   Protein

Exercise/Activity   Set / Reps   Time

....	....	....
....	....	....
....	....	....
....	....	....
....	....	....

Day (96)

Date ....

Mo Tu We Th Fr Sa Su

Breakfast	Lunch	Dinner
....	....	....
....	....	....
....	....	....
....	....	....
....	....	....
....	....	....
	....	....
Snacks	....	....
....	....	....
....	....	....
....	....	....
....	....	....
....	....	....

Total Calories
_____

Weight

Sleep   #Times Awake   Water   Protein

Exercise/Activity   Set / Reps   Time

....	....	....
....	....	....
....	....	....
....	....	....
....	....	....
....	....	....

Emotional State

Mo Tu We Th Fr Sa Su

Date ....

Day **97**

Breakfast	Lunch	Dinner
....	....	....
....	....	....
....	....	....
....	....	....
....	....	....
....	....	....
_____ ____	....	....
Snacks	....	....
....	....	....
....	....	....
....	....	....
....	....	....
....	....	....
_____ ____		_____ ____

Total Calories

_____

Weight

Sleep   #Times
            Awake

Water   Protein

Exercise/Activity   Set / Reps   Time

.... | .... | ....
.... | .... | ....
.... | .... | ....
.... | .... | ....
.... | .... | ....
.... | .... | ....

Day (98)

Mo Tu We Th Fr Sa Su

Date ....

Emotional State

○   ○   ○   ○

Breakfast	Lunch	Dinner
....	....	....
....	....	....
....	....	....
....	....	....
....	....	....
....	....	....
——————— ———	....	....
Snacks	....	....
....	....	....
....	....	....
....	....	....
....	....	....
....	....	....
——————— ———	——————— ———	——————— ———

Total Calories

———————————————

Weight

	Sleep	#Times Awake	Water	Protein
	....	....	....	....

Exercise/Activity   Set / Reps   Time

	Set / Reps	Time
....	....	....
....	....	....
....	....	....
....	....	....
....	....	....
....	....	....

Emotional State

Mo Tu We Th Fr Sa Su

Date ....

Day (99)

Breakfast	Lunch	Dinner
....	....	....
....	....	....
....	....	....
....	....	....
....	....	....
....	....	....
———— ——	....	....
Snacks	....	....
....	....	....
....	....	....
....	....	....
....	....	....
....	....	....
———— ——	———— ——	———— ——

Total Calories

————————

Weight

Sleep   #Times Awake   Water   Protein

Exercise/Activity   Set / Reps   Time

.... | .... | ....
.... | .... | ....
.... | .... | ....
.... | .... | ....
.... | .... | ....
.... | .... | ....

Day (100)

Mo Tu We Th Fr Sa Su

Date ....

Emotional State

Breakfast	Lunch	Dinner
....	....	....
....	....	....
....	....	....
....	....	....
....	....	....
....	....	....

Snacks

....	....	....
....	....	....
....	....	....
....	....	....
....	....	....

Total Calories

_____

Weight

Sleep   #Times Awake   Water   Protein

Exercise/Activity   Set / Reps   Time

....
....
....
....
....
....

My Measurements

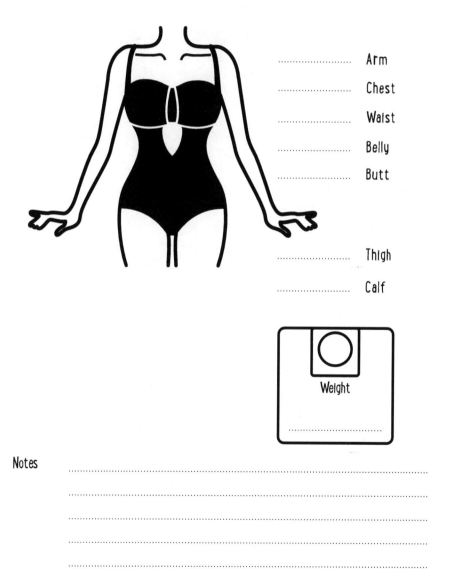

.... Arm

.... Chest

.... Waist

.... Belly

.... Butt

.... Thigh

.... Calf

Weight

....

Notes ....

....

....

....

....

Day **1**   Day **100**

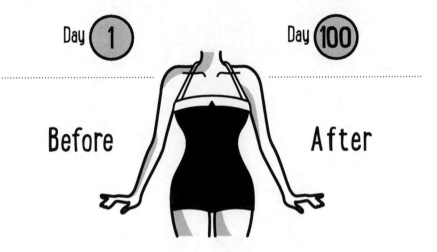

Before   # After

Arm	....	....	Arm
Chest	....	....	Chest
Waist	....	....	Waist
Belly	....	....	Belly
Butt	....	....	Butt
Thigh	....	....	Thigh
Calf	....	....	Calf

Weight Before

....

Weight After

....

Notes

....

....

....

....

....

....

....

....

....

....

....

....

....

....

....

....

....

....

....

Copyright © Creative Food Diary Ideas
Published by: Studio 5519, 1732 1st Ave #25519 New York, NY 10128
January 2017, Issue no. 1 (Version 1.0); Contact: info@studio5519.com; Date: January 9th 2017; Illustration credits: © StockUnlimited

Made in the USA
Lexington, KY
10 March 2018